For Liberty

THE STORY OF THE BOSTON MASSACRE

Addressed to the Inhabitants of America

Timothy Decker

CALKINS CREEK

Honesdale, Pennsylvania

Ｆrom 1753 until 1760, the nations of Great Britain and France waged war around the world.

The two empires fought over religion, politics, and natural resources.

The war drained both countries of men and money.

Unable to destroy each other, they agreed to a fragile peace.

The following years brought further hardship to Great Britain and its colonies.

The war produced a debt that had to be paid.

Parliament created new taxes as a solution to the problem.

The colonists in North America had no voice in Parliament but were required to obey its laws.

In Boston, some businessmen and tradesmen opposed the taxes.

Called the Sons of Liberty, they ruled the city through boycotts and riots.

Citizens loyal to the king were threatened and attacked.

British troops were sent to protect lives and property.

SONS OF LIBERTY!

DEFEND YOUR RIGHTS AND PROPERTY.

PAY NO
IMPORT DUTY.

BUY NO GOODS FROM LONDON.
BUY NOTHING FROM THE SELLERS

of Tea, Glass, Wine, Oil, Lead, Paint, etc.

Quarter no Fiendish Soldiers in Your Homes.
Welcome no Ill Bred Thieves to Your Hearth.

PROTECT YOUR LIBERTIES

in this Doleful and Dark Time.

By March 5, 1770, it was dangerous to be a soldier in Boston.

The mob swelled.
The reasonable men went home.
The bellicose remained.

A sentry saw Private White in distress and sought help from the officers of the 29th Regiment of Foot.

Aware of the unrest in the city, the officers discussed what action to take.
They could hear the growing din as they talked.

It was decided that Captain Preston would lead a group of soldiers to rescue Private White and

Captain Preston, Corporal Wemms, Private Carroll, Private Kilroy, Private Warren, Private Montgomery,

Shoving their way through the crowd, the soldiers reached Private White.
He joined their ranks.
Sensing the rising anger, Captain Preston tried to lead his men back to their barracks.

The throng of colonists grew as did the roar of their cries.
The angry crowd would not let the soldiers through.
Captain Preston ordered the soldiers to form a line near the corner of the Custom House.
Thus set, they could best defend the king's property and themselves.

The mob insulted the soldiers and dared them to fire.
They pelted the soldiers with snowballs, stones, and chunks of ice.

Captain Preston stood between his men and the colonists.
Surely the mob would not assault a trained soldier.
Surely his men would not fire for fear of shooting their officer.

Justice of the Peace James Murray hurried to King Street. He carried a copy of the Riot Act.
If he could read it to the crowd, they'd have to go home.
But tough men and angry boys blocked his path and threatened him.

Then, one of the missiles hit Private Montgomery and dropped him to the ground.

Pain and fear turned into rage.

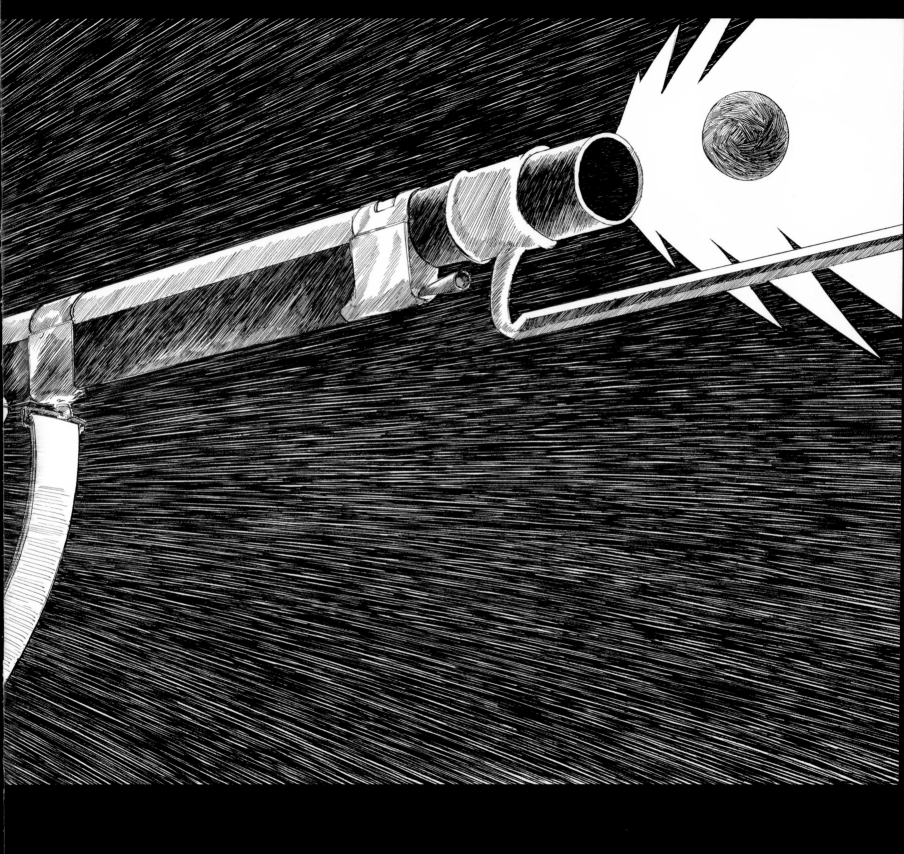

The shot surprised everyone.
Turning, Captain Preston lost his footing. As he fell, he was struck by a club.

A moment of silence descended over the street.
Preston sought protection behind his soldiers.

The night became a mix of shouting punctuated by explosions of musket fire.

After a few minutes of chaos, Captain Preston saw that his men were no longer in danger.

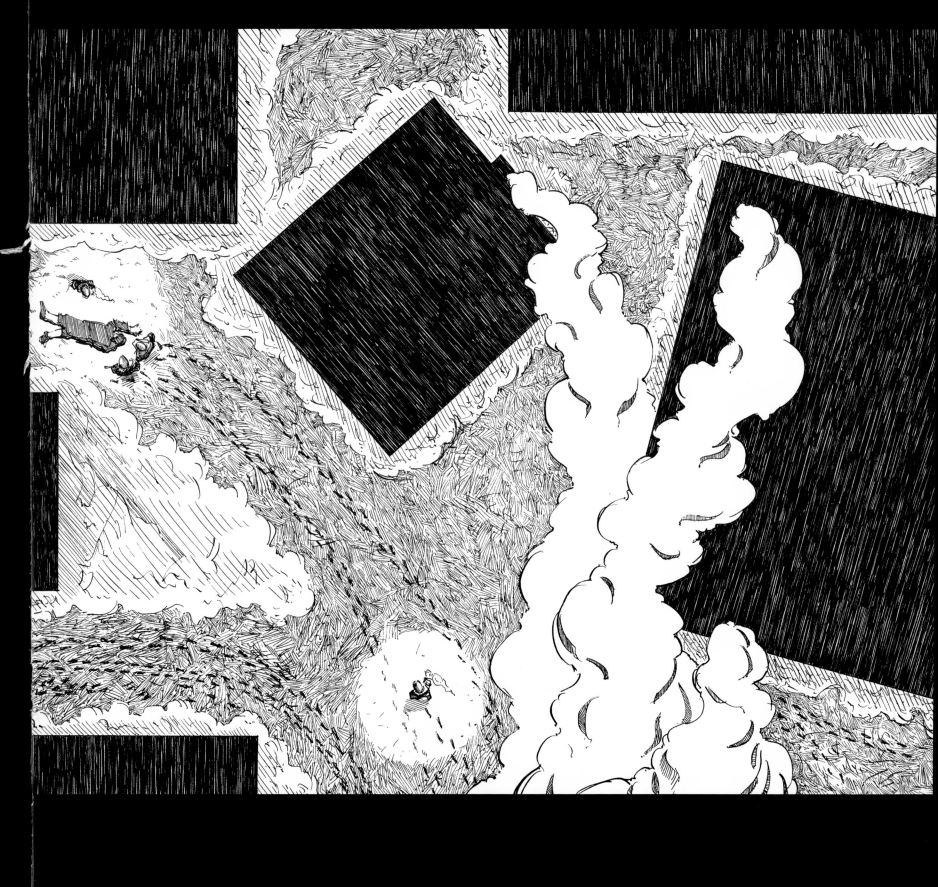

The sun rose on a changed city.

The soldiers were taken into custody and thus protected from the angry citizens. The rule of law demanded an investigation.

Lawyers were hired to prove that the soldiers provoked the riot. John Adams was chosen to lead the defense and prove that the soldiers were attacked.

The trial of Captain Preston began in October.

The story of the "massacre" was told before the court.

Witnesses spoke of the noise and confusion, the raised muskets and hurled stones.

But none could prove Captain Preston ordered his men to fire. He was found not guilty.

In November, the soldiers stood trial. John Adams spoke:

"… soldiers quartered in a populous town,
will always occasion two mobs, where they prevent one.
They are wretched conservators of the peace."

It was decided that the soldiers rightly defended their lives.
Most of the soldiers were found not guilty.
The two soldiers thought to have fired first were branded.

The Boston Massacre was the first in a series of conflicts between the Sons of Liberty and the agents of the king. Expensive tea was tossed into the harbor. Gunpowder and muskets were collected and hidden in the countryside. In time, all of the American colonies would challenge the power of British rule.

Eventually, there would be war.

John Adams foresaw a troubled future.

The lawless mob and the presence of soldiers were signs of a defective system of government.
He understood that no nation held dominion over liberty, the protection of one person from the actions
of another. He knew that liberty was precious and required wise, vigilant, and reasonable citizens to
protect it, even, at times, from the ignorance of one's own countrymen.